AI Audit Protection & IRS Defense

How Artificial Intelligence Reduces Your Risk of Being Audited

By Joe Correa

Published by Live Stronger Faster

This book is for educational and informational purposes only. The author and publisher are not engaged in rendering legal, financial, tax, or other professional advice. Readers should consult a qualified professional before making any financial decisions.

First Edition

Table of Contents

Introduction

Most taxpayers believe that audits are random, unpredictable, and mostly a matter of bad luck. In reality, nothing could be further from the truth. The modern IRS operates more like a data-driven intelligence agency than a paper-pushing bureaucracy. Every tax return you file is scanned, scored, compared, cross-referenced, and modeled against millions of other taxpayers using increasingly powerful algorithms. Patterns are identified. Anomalies are flagged. Risks are assigned. By the time a human IRS agent ever looks at a return, artificial intelligence has already decided how suspicious it is. In today's tax system, you are not audited by people first—you are audited by machines.

This shift has quietly transformed the tax landscape for individuals, small business owners, investors, gig workers, and even retirees. In the past, audits were triggered by crude rules: income too high, deductions too large, or a random selection. Today, IRS risk engines analyze hundreds of variables simultaneously. They compare your lifestyle to your income, your deductions to similar taxpayers, your industry to historical fraud patterns, and even your digital footprints across financial institutions. A tax return that looks "normal" to you may look statistically dangerous to an algorithm. That is why audits have become both more targeted and more devastating. The IRS no longer needs to audit many people—they only need to audit the right ones.

This is where artificial intelligence stops being a threat and becomes your greatest protection. The same technologies the IRS uses to detect risk can be used by taxpayers to eliminate it. AI systems can model how the IRS views your return before it is ever filed. They can simulate audit scores, detect red flags, and adjust reporting to stay within statistical safety zones. They can analyze deduction patterns, income ratios, filing history, and even audit trends across millions of similar taxpayers. What once required a team of forensic accountants is now available through intelligent software that works around the clock to keep you invisible to the IRS risk engines.

AI audit protection does not mean hiding income or cheating the system. In fact, it is the opposite. It means reporting everything accurately, but in a way that aligns with compliance algorithms rather than triggering them. The IRS is not just looking for fraud—it is looking for inconsistency, statistical outliers, and patterns that do not match your financial profile. AI helps you see those patterns before the IRS does. It shows you how to legally structure deductions, classify income, and present financial data in ways that fit within expected norms for your income level, profession, and geography.

One of the most dangerous myths in personal finance is that "if you are honest, you have nothing to worry about." Millions of honest taxpayers are audited every year not because they did anything illegal, but because their tax return looked unusual to an algorithm. A freelancer who suddenly claims large deductions, a homeowner who writes off a home office, a crypto investor with rapid trading volume, or a gig worker with fluctuating income can all appear risky even when everything is legitimate. AI audit protection exists to make your honesty look statistically normal rather than suspicious.

Artificial intelligence is especially powerful in predicting audit triggers because it processes tax data the same way the IRS does. It evaluates ratios, such as deductions relative to income, business expenses relative to revenue, charitable contributions relative to earnings, and losses relative to assets. It analyzes timing patterns, comparing year-over-year changes that might suggest manipulation. It even looks at the structure of your financial activity—how many accounts you use, how income flows between them, and how expenses are distributed. AI can flag risks that no human tax preparer would ever notice because the patterns only emerge across massive datasets.

What makes AI tax defense revolutionary is that it allows proactive protection instead of reactive panic. Traditionally, taxpayers only think about audits after they receive a letter from the IRS. By then, the system is already moving against them. AI changes this by simulating IRS scrutiny before you file. It allows you to run audit risk tests on your return, stress-test deductions, and identify weak points while there is still time to fix them. You are no longer guessing what the IRS might think—you can see it in advance.

This book will show you how artificial intelligence evaluates audit risk and how you can use that same intelligence to stay protected. You will learn how modern audit algorithms work, what patterns they look for, and how AI tools model those patterns. You will discover how to use AI to analyze your own tax profile, benchmark it against similar taxpayers, and make adjustments that dramatically lower your risk score without sacrificing legal tax savings. You will also learn how AI can prepare audit-ready documentation automatically, so that if the IRS ever does question you, you are already organized, compliant, and protected.

AI also transforms how taxpayers defend themselves once an audit begins. Instead of scrambling to find receipts, reconstruct income, or respond to confusing IRS letters, AI systems can instantly generate audit trails, categorize transactions, and produce clean, professional reports that satisfy IRS examiners. They can track deadlines, draft responses, and even predict which audit issues are most likely to be challenged. This dramatically shifts the balance of power. The IRS may have algorithms, but now so do you.

As digital payments, online platforms, and financial apps continue to grow, the IRS is collecting more data than ever before. Every bank account, payment processor, crypto exchange, employer, and gig platform reports information directly to the government. AI systems combine all of this into a detailed financial profile of every taxpayer. In this environment, the only safe way to operate is to understand how you are being modeled—and to use AI to shape that model in your favor. Taxpayers who ignore this reality will increasingly find themselves targeted, not because they did something wrong, but because their data did not fit neatly into an algorithm's expectations.

This book is not about fear. It is about control. AI gives you visibility into a system that was previously opaque. It allows you to see how your financial life appears to government algorithms and to adjust accordingly. It empowers you to file with confidence, knowing that your return has been optimized not just for savings, but for safety. In a world where machines decide who gets audited, it is only logical to fight machines with machines. By the time you finish this book, you will understand how AI-powered audit protection works, how to use it to defend yourself, and how to build a tax profile that stays compliant, invisible, and resilient year after year. You will no longer feel helpless before the IRS or uncertain about what might trigger an audit. You will be operating with the same intelligence that the system uses against you—except now it will be working for you.

Chapter 1

How the IRS Uses Artificial Intelligence to Select Audits

The Internal Revenue Service no longer relies on random chance or human intuition to decide who gets audited. Today, nearly every tax return filed in the United States is processed through multiple layers of artificial intelligence before a human ever sees it. These systems analyze income, deductions, expenses, assets, filing history, and even industry-specific behavior to determine how likely a taxpayer is to be misreporting something. The result is a numerical audit risk score that quietly determines whether your return moves forward untouched or gets flagged for further review. This means that in modern taxation, your financial life is evaluated first by machines, not by people.

At the heart of the IRS audit system are predictive models trained on decades of historical tax data. These models know what fraud looks like, what mistakes look like, and what honest taxpayers typically look like. When you file a return, the system compares your data against millions of others with similar income, location, profession, and financial behavior. If your deductions, losses, or income patterns fall outside of expected ranges, the system increases your audit risk. This happens automatically, silently, and instantly. Most taxpayers never realize their return was evaluated by multiple algorithms before it was accepted.

One of the most important factors in AI-based audit selection is pattern recognition. The IRS does not need proof of wrongdoing to start an audit. It only needs a pattern that looks unusual. For example, if self-employed individuals in your income bracket usually claim 12 to 18 percent of their income as business expenses, and you claim 45 percent, your return may be flagged. If rental property owners typically report small profits but you report large losses year after year, your return may be flagged. AI systems are extremely good at finding these kinds of statistical outliers, even when the numbers themselves are accurate.

Another powerful audit trigger comes from data matching. Every employer, bank, payment processor, and investment platform sends information directly to the IRS. W-2s, 1099s, K-1s, crypto transaction reports, and payment platform records are automatically compared to what you report on your tax return. If there is even a small mismatch, the system detects it instantly. AI does not forget, overlook, or ignore inconsistencies. A missing form, a rounding error, or a misclassified income stream can all raise your audit score. The IRS also uses AI to track behavioral changes over time. Sudden jumps in income, sharp increases in deductions, or dramatic changes in business activity can all trigger risk alerts. Even if the change is legitimate, it may look suspicious to an algorithm that is trained to detect fraud. A freelancer who suddenly starts making much more money, a crypto trader who becomes active after years of inactivity, or a homeowner who begins claiming a home office can all be flagged simply because their financial profile changed.

Industry-specific risk models also play a role. The IRS knows that certain professions have higher rates of underreporting or aggressive deductions. Cash-heavy businesses, gig workers, independent contractors, real estate investors, and crypto traders are all analyzed using specialized models designed for their financial behavior. These models know how money usually flows in those industries, how expenses are normally structured, and where fraud tends to occur. If your return does not fit the expected pattern for your profession, the AI system becomes suspicious.

What makes modern audit systems especially powerful is that they learn and adapt. Each audit that results in additional taxes, penalties, or criminal charges feeds more data back into the model. The AI becomes better at identifying what successful fraud looks like and how it hides itself. Over time, this makes the system more aggressive and more accurate. It also means that strategies that once worked to avoid audits may no longer be effective.

For taxpayers, this creates a new reality. You are not being evaluated against a fixed set of rules. You are being evaluated against constantly evolving statistical models. What looked normal last year may look risky this year because the AI has learned something new. This is why relying on outdated tax strategies or generic advice can be dangerous. The IRS is not just checking compliance; it is continuously refining its definition of what "suspicious" means.

This is where artificial intelligence on the taxpayer's side becomes essential. The same technology used by the IRS to detect risk can be used to reduce it. AI-powered tax tools can analyze your financial data the same way the IRS does. They can model audit risk, identify potential red flags, and suggest changes that keep you within safe statistical boundaries. Instead of guessing what might trigger an audit, you can see it in advance.

By understanding how the IRS uses AI, you gain the ability to protect yourself intelligently. You are no longer blindly filing and hoping for the best. You are using data, models, and predictive analysis to stay compliant, optimized, and invisible to the audit system. This is the foundation of modern tax defense, and it is the first step toward truly stress-free tax filing.

"The Algorithm That Almost Ruined Alex"

Alex never thought of himself as a risky taxpayer. He worked as a freelance web designer, paid his taxes every year, and used a popular online tax software to file his returns. When his income doubled after landing several high-paying clients, he felt proud. He also felt justified in writing off more expenses: software subscriptions, a new laptop, part of his rent for a home office, even some travel for client meetings. Everything was legitimate, so he didn't worry. He had no idea that somewhere inside an IRS server, his numbers were quietly lighting up like a warning sign.

When Alex filed his return, it was instantly processed by multiple AI systems. One model noticed that his deductions had jumped far more than the average freelancer in his income range. Another saw that his travel expenses were unusually high compared to others in his profession. A third model compared his income growth to historical patterns and decided it looked statistically unusual. None of these systems knew whether Alex had done anything wrong, but together they concluded that his return was risky. His audit score crossed a threshold, and without anyone making a conscious decision, his file was selected for review.

The letter arrived six weeks later. Alex opened it on a Tuesday morning and felt his stomach drop. The IRS was requesting documentation for his expenses, income, and deductions. They wanted bank statements, receipts, and explanations. He had never been audited before. Panic set in. He spent days digging through emails, credit card statements, and old files, trying to piece together a financial story that made sense. Everything was scattered. Nothing was organized. He suddenly realized how exposed he was.

A friend recommended an AI-powered tax defense platform that could reconstruct his financial history and prepare audit-ready reports. Desperate, Alex signed up. He connected his bank accounts, payment platforms, and accounting software. Within minutes, the system had categorized thousands of transactions, matched income to 1099 forms, and linked expenses to digital receipts. It generated clean reports that showed exactly where every dollar came from and where it went. It even identified which deductions were most likely to be questioned by the IRS and prepared explanations for them.

As Alex submitted the AI-generated reports to the IRS, something remarkable happened. The tone of the correspondence changed. The requests became narrower. The questions became more specific. The algorithm that had flagged him as risky was now seeing a clear, well-documented financial profile that matched legitimate business behavior. After several weeks, the audit was closed with no additional taxes owed. Alex felt an overwhelming sense of relief.

What he didn't know was that the same AI that saved him could have prevented the audit entirely. Had he used it before filing, it would have warned him that his expense ratios were outside normal ranges and suggested adjustments that would have lowered his risk score. It would have shown him how the IRS models freelancers like him and how to stay within safe boundaries without giving up legal deductions.

Alex learned a powerful lesson. In a world where algorithms decide who gets audited, protection comes from understanding those algorithms. He never filed another tax return without running it through AI first. The IRS still had its machines, but now he had his too—and for the first time, he felt truly in control.

Chapter 2

How AI Calculates Your Audit Risk Score

Every tax return filed in the modern system is quietly given a numerical identity long before any human ever reviews it. This identity is known as an audit risk score, and it determines whether your return passes through the IRS system unnoticed or is pulled aside for deeper scrutiny. While the IRS does not publish the exact formula, its structure is well understood by tax technologists and data scientists. It is built from hundreds of variables that measure how closely your financial life matches what the IRS expects for someone like you. Artificial intelligence analyzes these variables simultaneously, producing a probability that your return contains errors, omissions, or aggressive reporting.

The most powerful component of your audit risk score is statistical deviation. AI does not judge you based on morality or intent; it judges you based on how far you drift from normal behavior. The system groups taxpayers into profiles based on income level, location, profession, filing status, investment activity, and business ownership. Within each group, it learns what typical returns look like. When your deductions, credits, losses, or income flows deviate too far from those norms, your score increases. This is why two people claiming the same deduction may face very different audit risk depending on how their entire financial picture compares to others in their category.

Income consistency is another major factor. AI systems are highly sensitive to changes in earnings patterns. Sudden increases or drops in income, especially when they are not accompanied by clear documentation, raise risk flags. A freelance worker who suddenly doubles income, a real estate investor who reports large losses after years of profit, or a crypto trader who shows dramatic swings may all be statistically suspicious even when fully compliant. The AI is not accusing anyone of wrongdoing; it is simply reacting to patterns that historically correlate with errors or fraud.

Expense behavior is analyzed just as deeply. The IRS knows what types of expenses are typical for every profession. AI compares your reported expenses to those averages and to your own past behavior. If you suddenly begin claiming much higher travel, meals, or home office deductions, your audit score may rise. The system also looks at ratios, such as expenses relative to income, charitable donations relative to earnings, and business write-offs relative to revenue. These ratios are powerful predictors of audit interest because they reveal whether your financial story makes sense statistically.

Another layer of audit scoring comes from third-party reporting. Every W-2, 1099, brokerage statement, and payment processor report is matched against what you claim. Even small mismatches add risk points. If a payment platform reports income you forgot to include, or a brokerage sends a form that does not align with your return, the AI system sees it immediately. Over time, these mismatches compound, raising your overall score even if the dollar amounts are small.

Behavioral history also plays a role. Taxpayers who have previously been audited, adjusted, or penalized are statistically more likely to be reviewed again. AI incorporates this history into your profile. It also tracks filing habits, such as late filings, amended returns, or inconsistent reporting. These behaviors do not prove wrongdoing, but they make a return less predictable, which increases algorithmic risk.

What makes AI-based scoring so powerful is that it continuously learns. Each completed audit feeds back into the system. If a certain pattern frequently leads to additional taxes or penalties, the model assigns it more weight. If another pattern turns out to be harmless, its importance declines. This means audit risk is not static; it evolves. What was safe last year may not be safe this year, and what triggers audits today may change tomorrow. This is why traditional tax planning is no longer enough. You are no longer just complying with written tax law; you are interacting with invisible statistical models. AI-driven tax protection tools allow you to simulate how your return will be scored before you file. They can show you which deductions push you toward danger zones and which reporting choices lower your risk. This allows you to optimize both savings and safety, rather than sacrificing one for the other.

When you understand how your audit score is calculated, fear disappears. You stop wondering if you will be audited and start seeing how likely it is and why. This transforms tax filing from a gamble into a strategy. AI gives you the same lens the IRS uses, allowing you to position yourself intelligently inside the system instead of blindly hoping to avoid it.

"The Score That Saved Maria"

Maria had always prided herself on being careful with money. She ran a small online coaching business and earned a comfortable living helping clients improve their careers. When tax season came around, she hired a local accountant who did everything by the book. Still, Maria felt uneasy. Her income had grown quickly, and she had started deducting more expenses for software, marketing, and a home office. Everything was legitimate, but something about the numbers made her nervous. A fellow entrepreneur told her about an AI tax platform that could calculate audit risk. Curious, Maria uploaded her financial data. Within minutes, the system produced a report that shocked her. Her audit risk score was far higher than average for someone in her profession and income bracket. The AI showed her exactly why. Her advertising expenses were much higher than similar businesses. Her home office deduction was larger than typical. Her income growth rate looked abnormal compared to historical patterns.

None of these were illegal, but together they made her look like an outlier. The AI offered recommendations. It suggested restructuring some expenses, timing certain deductions differently, and improving documentation for others. It showed her how small changes could bring her back into safe statistical ranges without losing legitimate tax savings.

Maria followed the recommendations. When she re-ran the analysis, her audit risk dropped by more than half. The same income. The same expenses. But now her financial profile looked normal instead of suspicious. When she filed her return, it passed through the IRS system without triggering any alarms.

Months later, Maria received no audit letters, no questions, no requests for documents. She realized that AI had quietly done something powerful: it had allowed her to see herself the way the IRS saw her and to correct the story before it was judged. From that year forward, she never filed without checking her audit score first. For Maria, AI didn't just save money—it bought peace of mind.

Chapter 3

How AI Detects Red Flags Before the IRS Does

The most powerful advantage artificial intelligence gives taxpayers is not just the ability to calculate risk, but the ability to identify danger before it becomes visible to the IRS. Every audit begins with red flags—patterns, inconsistencies, or statistical anomalies that suggest something might be wrong. In the past, these flags were discovered only after a return had already been filed and selected. AI changes that by allowing taxpayers to scan their financial lives with the same lens used by government systems, exposing vulnerabilities while there is still time to correct them.

Red flags are not the same as errors. Many taxpayers assume that only mistakes or dishonesty trigger audits, but most red flags are simply signals that something looks unusual. A perfectly legal deduction can become a red flag if it is far larger than what similar taxpayers claim. A legitimate business loss can become a red flag if it happens too often or grows too quickly. AI excels at finding these patterns because it does not just look at your return—it looks at how your return compares to millions of others in your statistical category. One of the most common red flags involves mismatched data. Banks, employers, payment platforms, investment firms, and even crypto exchanges send data directly to the IRS. AI systems match this information against what you report. If income appears in one place but not another, or if totals do not align, the discrepancy is flagged. What makes this dangerous is that many mismatches come from innocent causes: delayed forms, platform reporting errors, or misclassified income. Without AI to catch these before filing, a taxpayer may never realize there is a problem until an audit begins.

Another powerful category of red flags comes from ratio analysis. AI constantly evaluates relationships between numbers. It looks at how much you earn relative to what you spend, how much you deduct relative to your income, and how your expenses are distributed. For example, if your charitable donations suddenly become a much larger percentage of your income, or your business expenses spike while revenue remains flat, the system notices. These ratios reveal stories about your financial behavior, and when the story looks unusual, the red flags appear.

Timing is also critical. AI models are extremely sensitive to when income and expenses occur. Sudden changes at the end of the year, large deductions taken all at once, or unusual clustering of transactions can raise suspicion. Even when everything is legal, patterns that resemble historical fraud or manipulation can be flagged. AI tools on the taxpayer side can analyze transaction timing and highlight areas where the pattern might look dangerous to IRS algorithms.

Industry-specific red flags add another layer of complexity. The IRS knows how money typically flows in different professions. A rideshare driver, a real estate investor, a crypto trader, and a freelance consultant all have different financial signatures. AI compares your financial behavior to others in your industry. If you claim expenses that are rare for your profession or report income in an unusual way, your profile stands out. AI-based tax tools use these same industry benchmarks to warn you when something looks out of place.

What makes red flag detection so valuable is that it gives you control. Instead of waiting to be questioned, you can proactively adjust, document, or restructure your reporting. AI might tell you that a deduction is technically legal but statistically risky. You can then decide whether to keep it, modify it, or strengthen its documentation. This turns tax filing into a strategic process rather than a gamble.

AI also creates a living audit defense file as you go. It links every income stream and expense to digital evidence. Receipts, bank statements, contracts, and invoices are automatically matched and stored. If a red flag cannot be eliminated, it can at least be fortified with proof. When the IRS sees a clean, well-documented trail, risk often dissolves before it turns into action.

In the modern tax system, the greatest danger is not breaking the law—it is being misunderstood by an algorithm. AI allows you to see how that algorithm interprets your financial story and to rewrite that story in a way that is both truthful and safe. By detecting red flags before the IRS does, you move from vulnerability to control, from fear to precision, and from reactive defense to proactive protection.

"The Warning That Changed Everything"

David had just sold his small e-commerce business. After years of building it, the payout felt like a victory. He invested part of the money, paid off debts, and claimed several deductions related to the sale. His accountant told him everything was legal, but something still felt uneasy. The numbers were big, and the changes to his financial profile were dramatic. A friend suggested he run everything through an AI tax analysis tool before filing.

When David uploaded his data, the results were unsettling. The AI flagged multiple red zones. His income spike from the business sale was far outside his historical pattern. His investment transfers created unusual cash flows. His deductions tied to the sale were statistically high compared to similar transactions. None of it was illegal, but together it painted a picture that looked risky to IRS algorithms.

The AI didn't just warn him—it explained why. It showed him how the IRS would see his return and which parts of his story looked unclear or abnormal. It suggested reorganizing how some income was reported, improving documentation for others, and spreading certain deductions across different reporting categories to match common patterns. It even simulated how each change would affect his audit risk.

David followed the guidance carefully. After adjusting and re-running the analysis, his red flags disappeared. His financial story now looked consistent, documented, and statistically normal. When he filed his return, it moved through the IRS system without triggering any alarms.

Months passed. No audit. No letters. No stress. David realized that the AI had done something no human ever could—it had shown him how invisible forces were judging his numbers and given him the power to respond. From that day on, he never trusted his financial story to chance. He let AI read it first.

Chapter 4

How AI Builds an Audit-Proof Financial Profile

The ultimate goal of AI audit protection is not merely avoiding red flags in a single tax year, but constructing a financial profile that remains consistently safe, defensible, and statistically normal over time. The IRS does not evaluate tax returns in isolation. Instead, it builds long-term profiles of taxpayers, tracking patterns, behaviors, ratios, and reporting consistency across years. Artificial intelligence allows taxpayers to do the same thing proactively, transforming tax compliance from a reactive annual event into a continuous system of protection.

An audit-proof financial profile begins with coherence. AI examines whether your income sources, expenses, deductions, and assets tell a logical story when viewed together. A return may be technically accurate but still appear suspicious if the narrative does not align. For example, reporting high income without corresponding lifestyle indicators, or claiming large deductions without consistent revenue growth, can raise questions. AI systems identify these narrative gaps by modeling how a complete financial picture should look for someone in your demographic, profession, and income range.

Consistency is one of the most heavily weighted factors in long-term audit risk. AI tracks how your numbers change year over year. Gradual growth looks normal. Sudden spikes or drops look risky. Repeated losses, fluctuating expense ratios, or inconsistent classifications can slowly elevate audit probability even if no single year appears alarming. AI-powered tax tools help smooth these patterns by forecasting how current decisions will affect future profiles, allowing taxpayers to make choices that remain defensible across multiple years rather than optimizing only for the present.

Documentation is another pillar of an audit-proof profile. AI systems automatically link transactions to evidence in real time. Instead of scrambling to reconstruct records during an audit, documentation is built as financial activity occurs. Every expense is categorized, justified, and supported. Every income stream is matched to source documents. This creates a digital audit trail that mirrors what IRS examiners expect to see. When AI builds this structure continuously, compliance becomes effortless rather than stressful.

AI also optimizes classification, one of the most underestimated sources of audit risk. Income misclassification, expense categorization errors, and improper reporting structures can all trigger scrutiny. AI analyzes how similar taxpayers classify their finances and flags deviations. This ensures that income appears where the IRS expects it, expenses are categorized appropriately, and deductions are positioned within accepted norms. Over time, this consistency reduces algorithmic suspicion.

Another key element is risk distribution. AI understands that certain deductions or financial activities carry higher audit sensitivity. Rather than eliminating these entirely, AI helps distribute risk intelligently. High-risk deductions can be supported with stronger documentation, offset by conservative reporting elsewhere, or timed strategically across years. This balance keeps the overall profile stable even when advanced tax strategies are used.

Perhaps most importantly, AI enables visibility. Most taxpayers do not know how they appear to IRS systems. AI makes that invisible evaluation visible. It shows risk trends, highlights emerging concerns, and alerts taxpayers when patterns begin to drift into dangerous territory. This early warning system allows course correction long before an audit is triggered.

An audit-proof profile is not about perfection. It is about predictability. The IRS trusts what it can predict. AI helps taxpayers become predictable in the best possible way—consistent, documented, logical, and aligned with statistical norms. When your financial profile fits cleanly within the models the IRS uses, audits become unlikely not by luck, but by design.

"The File the IRS Never Opened"

Ethan had always considered himself careful, but not strategic. He ran a small consulting firm, paid estimated taxes, and trusted his accountant to handle the details. Each year felt like a reset—new numbers, new forms, new stress. He never thought about how one year connected to the next, or how his financial life looked as a whole. To him, taxes were something you survived, not something you engineered.

That changed when his business began to grow quickly. New clients arrived. Income increased. Expenses followed. He upgraded software, hired contractors, traveled more, and started investing. Everything felt justified, yet something nagged at him. His numbers were changing fast, and he knew the IRS didn't like surprises. When a colleague mentioned AI-powered audit protection, Ethan was skeptical—but curious enough to try.

The first report startled him. The AI didn't accuse him of wrongdoing. It simply showed him his financial story as a system would see it. The year-over-year growth looked abrupt.

His contractor expenses were higher than average for similar firms. His deductions clustered heavily in one category. None of this was illegal, but together it made his profile unpredictable. The AI labeled it fragile.

Instead of panic, the system offered structure. It mapped his financial history across multiple years, identifying where consistency was missing. It recommended changes—not to hide income or reduce deductions, but to smooth patterns, improve categorization, and strengthen documentation. It explained how small shifts today could stabilize his profile for years to come.

Ethan followed the guidance. He restructured how he paid contractors. He documented business travel more thoroughly. He adjusted how expenses were categorized and timed. Each change barely affected his bottom line, but dramatically improved coherence. The AI updated his profile in real time, showing risk levels declining steadily.

The following year, something remarkable happened. Tax season arrived—and passed—with no anxiety. No second-guessing. No waiting for letters. His return flowed through the system without friction. The AI showed him why: his financial story now matched what the IRS expected to see from a growing consulting firm. He wasn't invisible—he was understandable.

Years passed. Ethan's business continued to grow. Investments expanded. Complexity increased. But audits never came. The AI tracked everything quietly in the background, adjusting, warning, optimizing. His tax filings became boring—and boring was perfect.

One day, while reviewing his dashboard, Ethan noticed a note: "Audit probability: extremely low." He smiled. Not because he feared the IRS anymore, but because he realized something profound. The most powerful defense wasn't secrecy or fear—it was clarity. His financial life made sense. And because it made sense, the IRS never had a reason to look closer.

The file was there. It always would be. But it was never opened.

Chapter 5

How AI Defends You During an Active IRS Audit

When an IRS audit begins, most taxpayers experience an immediate psychological shift. Fear replaces logic. Urgency replaces planning. The letter from the IRS may be short, but its impact is enormous. Questions flood the mind: What did I do wrong? What will they find? How much will this cost me? Artificial intelligence transforms this moment by replacing panic with precision. Instead of reacting emotionally, AI allows taxpayers to respond strategically, calmly, and with overwhelming clarity.

An active audit is not an accusation; it is an investigation triggered by statistical probability. The IRS already has a working theory when it contacts you. AI-powered audit defense begins by identifying that theory. By analyzing the audit notice, requested documents, and the tax year under review, AI systems can infer which patterns or red flags triggered scrutiny. This allows the response to be focused rather than scattered. Instead of oversharing or guessing, the taxpayer addresses exactly what the IRS is looking for. One of the most dangerous mistakes taxpayers make during audits is providing disorganized or excessive information. AI prevents this by structuring responses in the same logical framework the IRS uses internally. Every document is categorized, timestamped, cross-referenced, and tied directly to reported figures. Income is traced from source to bank deposit to tax return. Expenses are linked to receipts, business purpose, and classification logic. This creates a clean, professional audit package that reduces examiner confusion and shortens the audit timeline.

AI also manages communication strategy. Audits are conversations, not interrogations. The tone, timing, and structure of responses matter. AI systems track deadlines, recommend response pacing, and even draft audit letters using compliant language that avoids unnecessary admissions or ambiguity. This prevents taxpayers from unintentionally expanding the scope of the audit or introducing new areas of scrutiny.

Another critical advantage of AI is scenario modeling. Audits rarely end with a simple yes or no. They involve negotiation, clarification, and sometimes disagreement. AI can simulate multiple outcomes based on how different positions are defended. It can estimate potential adjustments, penalties, or outcomes before responses are submitted. This allows taxpayers to choose the strongest strategy rather than reacting blindly. Documentation strength becomes decisive during audits. AI evaluates not just whether documentation exists, but whether it is persuasive. It identifies weak points—missing receipts, vague descriptions, or inconsistent records—and recommends reinforcement where possible. In many cases, AI can reconstruct documentation using transaction metadata, bank records, and contextual evidence that human preparers might overlook.

Importantly, AI also helps taxpayers know when to stop. Over-defending low-risk items can raise suspicion. AI systems rank audit issues by sensitivity and likelihood of adjustment, guiding attention to where it matters most. This disciplined approach often results in faster resolutions and fewer follow-up requests.

An IRS audit is not won through confrontation or concealment. It is won through coherence. AI excels at coherence. It ensures that every number, explanation, and document tells the same story. When that story aligns with statistical norms and legal compliance, audits often resolve quietly and without escalation.

AI does not eliminate audits, but it neutralizes them. It shifts power back to the taxpayer by turning a stressful event into a managed process. With AI, an audit becomes a review—not a threat.

"The Audit That Never Escalated"

When the letter arrived, Laura didn't open it right away. She knew what it was. The envelope felt heavier than it should have, as if it carried more than paper inside. She had been expecting it ever since she filed her return. Her income had grown rapidly, her deductions were higher than ever, and deep down she knew she didn't fully understand how her financial story looked from the outside. She sat at her kitchen table for nearly an hour before finally tearing it open.

The audit notice was polite, almost sterile. A request for documentation. A list of items under review. A deadline. No accusations. No explanations. Just facts. Laura's heart raced anyway. She replayed the past year in her mind, wondering which decision had triggered this moment. The home office? The consulting income? The investment losses? Everything had seemed reasonable at the time, but now every number felt dangerous.

A friend urged her not to panic and recommended an AI-based audit defense platform. Skeptical but desperate, Laura signed up that same night. She uploaded the audit notice and connected her financial accounts. Within minutes, the system began assembling a complete picture of her financial life. It wasn't judging her—it was organizing her. The AI identified the most likely audit trigger: unusually high professional expenses relative to income growth. It showed her how the IRS likely interpreted her return and which items were drawing attention. Instead of guessing, Laura finally knew what she was defending. The AI didn't tell her to hide anything. It told her to explain everything clearly.

Over the next few days, the system guided her step by step. It reconstructed income flows from clients to deposits to reported figures. It matched expenses to receipts, emails, and contracts. It flagged weak documentation and helped her strengthen it using contextual data. Slowly, panic gave way to confidence.

When the response packet was ready, it was immaculate. Every number matched. Every explanation was concise. Every document had a purpose. Laura submitted it and waited.

Weeks passed. Then another letter arrived. This one was shorter. The IRS requested clarification on two minor items. The AI analyzed the request and advised a narrow response. No extra information. No unnecessary details. Laura followed the guidance exactly.

Another wait. Then silence.

Finally, a closing letter arrived. No adjustments. No penalties. No escalation. The audit was complete. Laura sat quietly after reading it, stunned by how uneventful the ending felt. What she had feared as a financial catastrophe had resolved almost peacefully. The AI dashboard showed her what had happened behind the scenes. Her documentation had reduced uncertainty. Her coherence had lowered risk. The system had done exactly what it was designed to do—make her understandable.

From that year on, Laura changed how she viewed taxes. She no longer saw audits as random threats. She saw them as conversations with systems—and systems could be managed. Each year, she let AI review her return before filing. She watched her audit risk shrink. And when tax season came, she felt something she never had before.

Calm.

The IRS still had its algorithms. But now, so did she.

Chapter 6

How AI Creates Long-Term IRS Immunity, Not Just Audit Avoidance

Avoiding a single audit is not the same as building lasting protection. Many taxpayers emerge from an audit relieved, only to unknowingly rebuild the same risk patterns that triggered scrutiny in the first place. Artificial intelligence changes this by shifting the goal from short-term survival to long-term immunity. Instead of reacting to IRS attention, AI helps taxpayers design financial lives that consistently fall outside audit priority zones year after year.

The IRS does not think in isolated moments. It thinks in trends. AI systems inside the agency track taxpayers across long timelines, learning who remains consistent, who drifts, and who repeatedly triggers uncertainty. Long-term immunity is built through predictability, not simplicity. A complex financial life can still be audit-resistant if it follows stable, explainable patterns. AI-powered tax systems help taxpayers identify and maintain those patterns regardless of income growth, investment expansion, or career changes.

One of the most powerful tools AI provides is longitudinal modeling. Rather than evaluating a single tax year, AI simulates how today's financial decisions affect future audit risk. It shows how deductions compound over time, how classification choices echo across years, and how income growth curves are interpreted by IRS models. This allows taxpayers to make decisions that remain defensible not just now, but five or ten years into the future.

Another key element of long-term immunity is behavioral alignment. AI analyzes how taxpayers interact with the system itself. Filing timing, consistency, amendment frequency, and reporting structure all become part of the profile. Taxpayers who behave predictably, file cleanly, and avoid erratic changes gradually fall into lower-risk categories. AI reinforces these behaviors automatically, nudging taxpayers toward patterns the IRS historically ignores.

AI also plays a crucial role in adapting to regulatory change. Tax law evolves constantly, and outdated strategies can quickly become risky. AI systems update continuously, adjusting guidance as IRS enforcement priorities shift. This ensures that tax strategies remain aligned with current rules and enforcement focus rather than relying on static advice that may no longer be safe.

Over time, AI transforms tax compliance into an invisible background process. Instead of stressful annual events, tax optimization becomes continuous and automatic. Risk is monitored. Patterns are adjusted. Documentation is maintained. The taxpayer's profile becomes so consistent and transparent that audits become statistically unlikely—not because income is low or activity is minimal, but because the system sees no uncertainty worth investigating.

True IRS immunity is not secrecy. It is clarity sustained over time. AI makes that clarity possible at scale, ensuring that even as financial lives grow more complex, they remain predictable to the systems that judge them.

"The Decade the IRS Forgot"

When Marcus started his business, taxes were an afterthought. He was focused on survival—getting clients, paying bills, keeping the lights on. His first few tax returns were rushed, imperfect, and stressful. He paid what he owed, but never felt confident. Each year felt like a gamble. He assumed that eventually, the IRS would come knocking.

As the business grew, so did the anxiety. New income streams appeared. Investments followed. Complexity multiplied. Marcus knew that the more successful he became, the more visible he would be. He told himself he would "fix it later," unaware that every year was quietly shaping a long-term profile he couldn't see.

The wake-up call came when a colleague mentioned being audited twice in five years. The pattern terrified Marcus. He realized audits weren't random—they were cumulative. That night, he searched for answers and discovered AI-driven tax optimization. It sounded futuristic, almost excessive, but something about the idea stuck with him. Not avoidance. Immunity.

The first AI report was uncomfortable. It showed inconsistencies across years. Expense ratios that drifted. Income classifications that shifted without explanation. None of it was illegal, but together it painted a picture of unpredictability. Marcus felt exposed—not to the IRS, but to his own lack of structure.

Instead of judgment, the AI offered a roadmap. It showed him how the IRS likely viewed his trajectory. It explained how small adjustments now could stabilize his profile over time. It didn't promise miracles. It promised discipline.

Year one was about cleanup. Reclassification. Documentation. Alignment. Marcus followed the guidance carefully, resisting the urge to optimize aggressively. The AI tracked his risk trend, and slowly, it began to flatten.

Year two brought growth. More clients. Higher income. More deductions. This time, nothing felt rushed. The AI guided every decision, showing Marcus how each choice affected his long-term profile. When he filed, the system showed a declining audit probability.

Year three passed quietly. Then year four. Then five.

Marcus stopped thinking about audits. Not because he forgot the IRS existed, but because his dashboard told him something remarkable. His profile had stabilized. His financial story made sense—year after year. Income rose gradually. Expenses followed predictable patterns. Investments were documented cleanly. Nothing stood out.

A decade passed.

One evening, Marcus reviewed his history out of curiosity. Ten years. No audits. No letters. No questions. His AI system showed him why. His profile had fallen into a category the IRS rarely touched—not because it was small, but because it was boring. Predictable. Coherent.

Marcus laughed quietly. He had built a complex, successful financial life—and the IRS had effectively forgotten him.

That was the real power of AI. Not fear. Not secrecy. Just understanding.

The IRS still had its machines.

But they had moved on.

Chapter 7

How AI Turns Tax Compliance Into a Silent, Automatic Defense System

The final evolution of AI audit protection is invisibility through automation. At this stage, taxpayers are no longer actively "avoiding audits" or "defending themselves." Instead, compliance becomes a silent, continuous system operating in the background of daily life. Artificial intelligence transforms tax defense from an annual event into an always-on shield that constantly monitors risk, adjusts patterns, and reinforces compliance without requiring constant attention. This is the point where taxes stop being stressful and start becoming predictable.

Traditional tax compliance is episodic. People gather documents once a year, rush through decisions, and hope for the best. AI replaces this with continuous awareness. Every transaction, income stream, expense, and classification choice is evaluated in real time. AI systems monitor how financial behavior evolves month by month, comparing it to long-term models and industry benchmarks. When patterns begin drifting toward risk, the system alerts the taxpayer early—long before those patterns ever appear on a tax return. This automation is critical because most audit risk is not created by single decisions, but by accumulation. Small inconsistencies compound. Minor classification errors repeat. Expense ratios drift slowly. Humans rarely notice these changes until they become problems. AI notices immediately. It tracks micro-trends across years, identifying subtle shifts that might eventually raise IRS suspicion. By correcting course early, AI prevents risk from ever forming.

Another advantage of automated defense is emotional neutrality. Humans make tax decisions under pressure—end-of-year deadlines, cash flow stress, fear of owing money. AI does not experience stress. It evaluates decisions objectively, recommending actions that balance legality, optimization, and long-term safety. This removes impulsive behavior from tax planning, replacing it with disciplined consistency.

Automation also standardizes documentation. Instead of scrambling to justify expenses retroactively, AI builds evidence as transactions occur. Receipts are matched instantly. Business purposes are logged automatically. Income sources are categorized cleanly. This creates a living audit file that is always complete. If the IRS ever requests information, the response is immediate and coherent, not rushed or reconstructed.

Perhaps the most powerful aspect of automated defense is behavioral signaling. The IRS does not just evaluate numbers—it evaluates reliability. Taxpayers who file consistently, respond predictably, and maintain stable reporting patterns are statistically less interesting. AI helps taxpayers send those signals year after year. Over time, this reliability compounds into algorithmic trust.

Eventually, something subtle happens. The taxpayer stops thinking about audits entirely. Not out of ignorance, but because the system has proven itself repeatedly. Returns are filed confidently. Letters never arrive. The tax system fades into the background where it belongs.

This is the true promise of AI audit protection—not fear reduction, but mental freedom. When compliance becomes automatic, life becomes lighter.

"The Year Taxes Stopped Existing"

For most of her adult life, taxes lived rent-free in Natalie's head. Not constantly, but persistently. A low-level hum of anxiety that never fully disappeared. Every purchase sparked a question. Every deduction carried doubt. Every filing season arrived with tension. She wasn't dishonest. She wasn't careless. She was simply human—and humans are not designed to interpret invisible systems judging them silently.

Natalie ran a growing digital marketing agency. Her income fluctuated. Her expenses evolved. Her life changed faster than her understanding of how the IRS perceived those changes. Each year, she told herself she would "get better organized next time." And each year, she survived tax season and moved on—until the next wave of stress arrived.

The turning point wasn't an audit. It was exhaustion.

Late one night, while reviewing expenses for the third time in a week, Natalie realized she wasn't afraid of the IRS itself. She was afraid of not knowing. Afraid that somewhere, quietly, something was being misunderstood. That fear was heavier than any tax bill.

She found AI tax automation almost by accident. At first, it felt unnecessary—like insurance she hoped never to need. But curiosity won. She connected her accounts. Uploaded history. Let the system analyze her financial life.

The first insight wasn't about money. It was about patterns. The AI showed her how her financial behavior looked across time. Where it was consistent. Where it drifted. Where it quietly accumulated risk. None of it was dramatic. That was the point. Risk was forming invisibly.

The AI didn't demand action. It adjusted quietly. Categorized automatically. Logged documentation as transactions occurred. Alerted her gently when something looked unusual. Suggested changes early—before urgency or fear appeared.

Weeks passed. Then months.

Natalie noticed something strange. She stopped thinking about taxes. Not deliberately. They simply stopped demanding attention. Receipts were handled. Income was tracked. Patterns were stable. The system worked in the background like electricity—unseen but essential.

The next tax season arrived without announcement. No stress. No dread. Filing took minutes. The AI confirmed her risk profile was stable and low. When she clicked submit, there was no lingering fear.

Then nothing happened.

No letters. No follow-ups. No waiting.

A year passed. Then another.

One afternoon, Natalie realized she couldn't remember the last time she worried about taxes. Not because she was careless—but because she trusted the system. Compliance had become invisible.

Taxes hadn't disappeared.

But they no longer existed in her mind.

And that, she realized, was freedom.

Chapter 8

How AI Handles Complex Lives, Multiple Income Streams, and High Visibility Tax Profiles

As financial lives become more complex, audit risk does not increase because of wrongdoing—it increases because of misunderstanding. The IRS is not designed to interpret nuance gracefully. It relies on models that expect consistency, categorization, and predictable structure. When a taxpayer's life includes multiple income streams, investments, business entities, digital platforms, or geographic exposure, the chance of misinterpretation grows exponentially. Artificial intelligence exists to translate complexity into clarity before that misinterpretation ever occurs.

High-visibility tax profiles are created when income flows from many directions. Salary combined with consulting. Consulting combined with investments. Investments combined with real estate. Real estate combined with digital assets. Each additional stream adds friction to the IRS's understanding. AI does not simplify life by removing complexity; it organizes complexity so that it appears logical rather than chaotic. This distinction is critical. The IRS does not penalize complexity—it penalizes uncertainty.

One of the most common risks for complex taxpayers is fragmentation. Income may be reported correctly in total but inconsistently in structure. Expenses may be legitimate but scattered across categories. Timing may be accurate but clustered in ways that resemble manipulation. AI systems specialize in unifying fragmented data into a single coherent narrative. They map how money flows across accounts, entities, platforms, and time. They ensure that each component reinforces the same story rather than contradicting it.

Multiple income streams also introduce classification risk. The same dollar can be treated very differently depending on how it is labeled. Earned income, passive income, investment income, and business income are all evaluated through different IRS lenses. AI ensures that classification decisions remain consistent across years and aligned with how similar taxpayers report comparable activity. This prevents category drift, one of the most subtle and dangerous long-term audit triggers.

Visibility is another underestimated factor. As income rises, as public presence grows, or as business scale increases, the IRS pays closer attention—not out of suspicion, but out of probability. Larger financial footprints create more data, more reporting sources, and more chances for discrepancy. AI acts as a coordination layer, reconciling third-party reports with internal records automatically. This ensures that visibility does not translate into vulnerability.

AI also manages entity complexity. Taxpayers with LLCs, partnerships, trusts, or multiple businesses face heightened risk if entities overlap inconsistently. AI systems analyze inter-entity transactions, ownership structures, and reporting symmetry. They identify where boundaries blur and reinforce separation where needed. This protects against both audits and reclassification risk.

Ultimately, AI allows complex taxpayers to scale safely. It ensures that growth does not amplify audit exposure. Instead of becoming more visible to enforcement systems, the taxpayer becomes more understandable. Complexity remains—but confusion disappears.

This is the difference between being noticed and being investigated. AI ensures that even the most complex financial lives remain audit-resistant by design.

"Too Many Streams to Count"

By the time Jonathan turned forty-five, his life no longer fit into a single box. He had a consulting firm. Two online businesses. Rental properties in three states. Investment accounts spread across platforms. Occasional speaking income. Royalties from a book he'd written years earlier. On paper, everything added up. In practice, it felt like a fragile balancing act.

Jonathan wasn't reckless. He paid his taxes. He hired professionals. But each year felt heavier. More documents. More explanations. More anxiety. He sensed that his financial life had become difficult to interpret—not just for him, but for anyone else trying to understand it. Especially the IRS.

The fear wasn't irrational. Friends with far simpler lives had been audited. Jonathan imagined what an audit of his situation would look like. Dozens of accounts. Thousands of transactions. Years of complexity. The thought alone was exhausting.

The breaking point came during tax preparation one winter evening. His accountant asked a simple question: "How do you want to classify this income?" Jonathan realized he didn't know. Not because it was wrong—but because the line between categories had blurred over time. That uncertainty scared him more than any tax bill.

That night, he explored AI-driven tax organization. Not optimization. Organization.

The first analysis was sobering. The AI showed him how fragmented his financial story appeared. Income streams that didn't clearly connect. Expense categories that shifted subtly year to year. Timing patterns that made sense to a human—but not to an algorithm. Nothing was illegal. Everything was explainable. But explanation requires clarity, and clarity was missing.

Instead of overwhelming him, the AI began stitching things together. It mapped income flows visually. Showed how each stream related to others. Identified where classification drift had occurred and recommended alignment. It didn't force simplification. It created structure.

Over the next year, Jonathan changed nothing about how he lived or earned. He simply allowed AI to coordinate it all. Accounts were reconciled automatically. Income streams were categorized consistently. Entity boundaries were reinforced. Documentation was generated continuously.

When tax season arrived, something unexpected happened. There was no chaos. No frantic searching. No confusion. The AI presented a clean, unified financial narrative. Jonathan reviewed it—not with fear, but with curiosity. For the first time, his life made sense on paper.

He filed.

Then waited.

Nothing happened.

Months passed. Then years.

Jonathan's income grew. His investments expanded. His complexity increased. But the system scaled with him. Each new stream was integrated seamlessly. Each new entity reinforced structure rather than eroding it.

One afternoon, Jonathan received an IRS notice. His heart skipped. He opened it carefully.

It wasn't an audit.

It was a generic informational update.

He laughed out loud—relieved not because he feared an audit, but because he realized something profound. His complexity no longer made him fragile. It made him robust—because it was understood.

AI hadn't hidden him.

It had explained him.

And in a system driven by algorithms, explanation was protection.

Chapter 9

How AI Prevents Small Mistakes From Becoming Life-Altering IRS Problems

Most tax disasters do not begin with fraud. They begin with small mistakes. A misclassified expense. An omitted form. A misunderstood reporting rule. A timing error. On their own, these mistakes seem insignificant. But within the IRS system, small errors compound quickly. Artificial intelligence exists to stop that chain reaction before it ever starts, transforming minor issues into quiet corrections instead of escalating crises.

The IRS operates on accumulation. One error may trigger a notice. A second creates a pattern. A third establishes risk. AI-powered enforcement systems are designed to detect not just wrongdoing, but repetition. Taxpayers who repeatedly file returns requiring adjustment—even minor ones—are statistically more likely to be audited in the future. AI tax protection works by eliminating repeat friction, ensuring that small mistakes do not become behavioral signals that draw long-term scrutiny.

One of the most common sources of escalation is misunderstanding complexity. As financial lives evolve, tax rules multiply. New income types bring new reporting requirements. New investments introduce unfamiliar forms. New platforms report data differently. Humans miss details. AI does not. AI systems track rule changes, reporting thresholds, and documentation requirements automatically, alerting taxpayers before errors occur rather than after penalties are assessed.

Another dangerous escalation point is response behavior. When taxpayers receive IRS notices, many respond incorrectly—not because they are hiding anything, but because they are confused. They overshare. Undershare. Miss deadlines. Or respond emotionally. AI removes emotion from the process. It interprets notices, identifies intent, and guides precise responses that resolve issues without expanding scrutiny. This alone prevents countless minor problems from becoming full audits.

AI also prevents silent errors—mistakes that go unnoticed for years. Misclassifications that persist. Basis errors that grow. Depreciation issues that compound. These are particularly dangerous because they build quietly, often surfacing only when the IRS performs a deeper review. AI audits financial history continuously, identifying drift and correcting course early.

Most importantly, AI reframes compliance as maintenance rather than defense. Instead of reacting to mistakes, taxpayers maintain clean systems. Errors are corrected quietly. Patterns remain stable. Nothing escalates.

In the IRS system, escalation is not inevitable. It is preventable. AI ensures that small mistakes stay small—and often disappear entirely.

"The Letter That Changed Nothing"

The letter arrived on a Thursday.

It wasn't thick. It wasn't threatening. It didn't use bold language or alarming phrases. It was just an IRS notice—plain, neutral, informational. Years ago, it would have ruined Daniel's week. Maybe his month. This time, it barely slowed him down.

Daniel noticed the envelope while sorting mail after dinner. He recognized it instantly. The logo. The formatting. The subtle weight of authority. A decade earlier, a letter like this had sent his pulse racing. Back then, he would have replayed every financial decision he'd made, searching for mistakes. But tonight, something was different.

He opened it calmly.

The notice explained that one form attached to his prior return did not match third-party reporting exactly. A small discrepancy. A timing issue. No accusation. Just a request for clarification.

Daniel smiled faintly.

He remembered a time when something this minor would have consumed him. He would have panicked, dug through old files, guessed at explanations, and probably made the situation worse by responding too quickly or too broadly. That version of Daniel no longer existed.

He logged into his AI tax system.

The platform had already flagged the issue weeks earlier. A delayed reporting form from an investment platform had arrived after he filed. The AI had noted the mismatch and prepared a reconciliation automatically. Documentation was already organized. The explanation was drafted—concise, accurate, unemotional.

Daniel reviewed it, approved it, and submitted the response.

Total time: twelve minutes.

He closed his laptop and returned to his evening.

A week passed.

Then two. Then nothing.

Years earlier, Daniel had learned the hard way how small mistakes escalate. He had once misclassified a modest income stream. It wasn't intentional. He simply didn't understand how it should be reported. The IRS caught it. He responded poorly—too much explanation, too little clarity. That led to follow-up questions. Those questions uncovered another small inconsistency. Within months, a minor error had turned into a full audit.

The stress had been brutal. Not because he owed money—but because he felt powerless. Every response felt like a guess. Every letter felt ominous.

That experience changed him.

He adopted AI tax oversight not because he feared the IRS—but because he wanted certainty. Over time, the system corrected small errors quietly. It prevented drift. It caught issues early. Notices became rare. When they arrived, they were handled effortlessly.

Daniel realized something most people never do: the IRS is not hunting individuals—it is managing uncertainty. When uncertainty disappears, attention fades.

That Thursday night, as he finished his tea, Daniel reflected on how anticlimactic the notice had been. It hadn't disrupted his sleep. It hadn't altered his plans. It hadn't even lingered in his thoughts.

The mistake had existed.

But it hadn't mattered.

Because it hadn't escalated.

That was the real power of AI—not perfection, but containment.

Small problems stayed small.

And life went on uninterrupted.

Chapter 10

The End of Fear: How AI Redefines Your Relationship With the IRS Forever

The final transformation AI brings to tax compliance is not technical—it is psychological. For decades, the IRS has occupied a unique space in the minds of taxpayers: distant, powerful, opaque, and unpredictable. Even those who follow the rules often carry a quiet fear that something could go wrong. Artificial intelligence ends this dynamic by replacing uncertainty with understanding. When taxpayers can see how they are evaluated, fear loses its grip.

The IRS is not an adversary. It is a system designed to manage scale. Millions of returns, trillions of dollars, and limited human oversight require automation. AI does not make the IRS more hostile; it makes it more systematic. Problems arise only when taxpayers remain blind to how that system interprets them. AI on the taxpayer's side removes that blindness.

Over time, AI shifts tax compliance from an external threat to an internal process. Instead of wondering whether you are "safe," you can measure it. Instead of guessing what might trigger scrutiny, you can see it. Instead of reacting defensively, you can act proactively. This reframing dissolves anxiety not through reassurance, but through control.

The long-term impact of this shift cannot be overstated. Taxpayers who understand the system stop making fear-based decisions. They stop avoiding legal deductions out of anxiety. They stop rushing filings. They stop treating the IRS as an unpredictable force. Instead, they operate within clear parameters, confident that their financial story makes sense.

AI also restores balance. Historically, only large corporations had access to sophisticated audit defense, predictive modeling, and continuous compliance systems. AI democratizes that power. Individuals, freelancers, investors, and small business owners can now operate with the same level of foresight and protection once reserved for enterprises with legal departments.

Ultimately, AI changes the question taxpayers ask. It is no longer “Will I get audited?” It becomes “How stable is my profile?” That question is answerable. Measurable. Manageable.

When fear disappears, compliance becomes calm. When compliance becomes calm, financial decisions improve. And when financial decisions improve, wealth grows without stress.

This is not the future of taxes.

This is the end of fear around them.

"The Last Time He Ever Feared the IRS"

There was a time when Thomas believed the IRS was always watching him.

Not in a dramatic way. Not paranoia. Just a quiet awareness that never fully left. When he earned more, he worried. When he deducted expenses, he hesitated. When he filed his return, he held his breath. The fear wasn't constant—but it was persistent, like background noise you only notice when it stops.

Thomas had done well for himself. A successful career. Investments. A side business that grew into something meaningful. By most standards, he was financially responsible. But responsibility didn't bring peace. It brought more questions.

Each year, tax season felt heavier. More forms. More rules. More things that could go wrong. He hired professionals, but even they couldn't answer the question that haunted him: *How does the IRS see me?*

No one could tell him that.

Until AI did. Thomas didn't adopt AI tax protection because of an audit. He adopted it because of a realization. He was making decisions in the dark, and darkness breeds fear. He wanted light.

The first time the AI analyzed his profile, Thomas felt exposed. Not judged—*seen*. The system showed him patterns across years. Where his income grew unevenly. Where his deductions clustered. Where classification drifted subtly. None of it was alarming, but together it formed a narrative that wasn't as clean as he'd assumed.

Instead of panic, something unexpected happened.

Relief.

For the first time, the uncertainty had shape. It was measurable. Fixable.

Over the next year, Thomas didn't change his life. He changed his awareness. The AI tracked everything quietly. Adjusted gently. Warned early. Explained patiently. Tax decisions became deliberate instead of anxious.

When filing season came, Thomas felt...nothing.

No tension. No second-guessing. No waiting for the other shoe to drop.

He filed. Weeks passed.

Nothing.

Months passed.

Nothing.

Years passed.

Still nothing.

One evening, Thomas found an old folder on his computer labeled “Taxes – Backup.” Inside were years of spreadsheets, notes, scanned receipts, and half-finished explanations. Artifacts of anxiety. He realized he hadn’t opened that folder in years.

The fear was gone.

Not because he ignored the IRS.

But because he understood it.

AI hadn’t made him invisible. It had made him clear. Predictable. Boring to the system that once frightened him.

Thomas closed the folder and deleted it.

Not out of defiance.

Out of closure.

That was the last time he ever feared the IRS.

Final Thoughts

The Quiet Power of Being Understood

For most people, the fear of the IRS is not rooted in wrongdoing. It is rooted in uncertainty. It is the discomfort of knowing that powerful systems are evaluating your financial life without explanation, without transparency, and without context. You may follow the rules, file honestly, and still feel exposed. That feeling does not come from guilt—it comes from not knowing how you are being interpreted. This book exists to resolve that uncertainty.

Throughout these chapters, one truth has become clear: the IRS does not operate on intuition or emotion. It operates on probability, pattern recognition, and statistical modeling. Audits are not personal. They are not moral judgments. They are outcomes generated by systems designed to manage scale. When taxpayers understand this, fear loses its mystique. What once felt unpredictable becomes measurable. What once felt threatening becomes navigable.

Artificial intelligence is not changing tax enforcement—it is revealing it. The same tools that the IRS uses to identify risk can now be used by taxpayers to eliminate it. This shift is profound. It marks the end of blind compliance and the beginning of informed participation. When you can see how your financial story appears to enforcement systems, you can shape that story intelligently rather than defensively.

The greatest misconception about audit protection is that it requires secrecy, minimalism, or restraint. In reality, it requires clarity. The IRS does not pursue complexity—it pursues confusion. AI allows complexity to exist without confusion. Multiple income streams, growing investments, evolving careers, and expanding businesses can all coexist safely when they are organized, documented, and consistent. AI does not remove opportunity; it protects it.

Another quiet transformation introduced by AI is emotional freedom. Tax stress consumes mental energy far beyond its financial cost. Worrying about audits, notices, mistakes, or unknown risks distracts from building wealth, enjoying success, and planning the future. When AI removes uncertainty, it also removes emotional weight. Compliance becomes background noise instead of a recurring source of anxiety.

This book has shown that audits are not sudden disasters. They are outcomes of accumulated signals. AI prevents those signals from forming. Small mistakes are corrected early.

Patterns remain stable. Documentation stays current. Over time, the IRS sees fewer reasons to engage. Not because you are hidden—but because you are understood.

Perhaps the most important lesson is this: tax compliance is no longer about avoiding attention. It is about earning algorithmic trust. Systems ignore what they can predict. AI helps you become predictable in the best possible way—consistent, logical, and statistically normal, even as your financial life grows.

As you close this book, the goal is not that you fear the IRS less. The goal is that you stop fearing it at all—not through denial, but through mastery. When you understand how the system works, it stops feeling powerful over you. It becomes something you navigate calmly and confidently.

This is not just audit protection.

This is peace of mind, engineered.

www.ingramcontent.com/pod-product-compliance
Lightning Source LLC
LaVergne TN
LVHW022025200926
848481LV00007B/2546

* 9 7 9 8 2 9 5 5 7 6 8 0 5 *